M. F. Rowe

**The Master's Messenger**

Or, Gospel truths in rhyme: collection of spiritual songs and short poems, principally devoted to the subject of scriptural holiness

M. F. Rowe

**The Master's Messenger**
*Or, Gospel truths in rhyme: collection of spiritual songs and short poems, principally devoted to the subject of scriptural holiness*

ISBN/EAN: 9783337394721

Printed in Europe, USA, Canada, Australia, Japan

Cover: Foto ©Lupo / pixelio.de

More available books at **www.hansebooks.com**

# THE
# MASTER'S MESSENGER,

OR,

# GOSPEL TRUTHS IN RHYME.

COLLECTION OF SPIRITUAL SONGS AND SHORT POEMS, PRINCIPALLY DEVOTED TO THE SUBJECT OF SCRIPTURAL HOLINESS.

BY

MRS. M. F. ROWE,

GRASS VALLEY, CAL.

---

San Francisco:
JOS. WINTERBURN & CO., PRINTERS AND ELECTROTYPERS.
1884.

# DEDICATION.

TO MY ESTEEMED FRIEND AND FORMER PASTOR,

REV. GEORGE NEWTON,

LEADER OF THE HOLINESS WORK ON THE PACIFIC COAST,

THIS LITTLE BOOK IS RESPECTFULLY DEDICATED

BY HIS CHILD IN THE GOSPEL,

M. F. ROWE.

# INTRODUCTION.

> "A verse may find him who a sermon flies,
> And turn delight into a sacrifice."

So wrote the poet Herbert, and Lowell said:

> "Never did Poesy appear
> So full of heaven to me, as when
> I saw how it would pierce through pride and fear
> To the lives of coarsest men."

So goes this little book, on a mission which Poetry alone can accomplish, a work for the good of man, for the glory of God, a work of love in the warfare with sin. It goes with many a prayer that God will give success, prayers sent up by those who know

> "'That no success attends on spears and swords
> Unblest, and that the battle is the Lord's."

Dear Reader, may you be lifted nearer the throne by the persual of these lines. Remember that these are not sketches of the fancy. They are the expression of one of those concerning whom it is written,

> "Poets are all who love—who feel great truths,
> And tell them."

M. D. BUCK.

GRASS VALLEY, CAL., July 16, 1884.

# CONTENTS.

|     |                                      | PAGE. |
|-----|--------------------------------------|-------|
| 1.  | Dedication                           | 3     |
| 2.  | Introduction, by Rev. M. D. Buck,    | 5     |
| 3.  | The Little Messenger,                | 9     |
| 4.  | Walking in the Light,                | 11    |
| 5.  | Rest,                                | 13    |
| 6.  | The Three Gifts,                     | 15    |
| 7.  | Son or Servant, Which?               | 17    |
| 8.  | The Child's Answer,                  | 19    |
| 9.  | Sanctified and Satisfied,            | 21    |
| 10. | The Anchor Within the Veil,          | 23    |
| 11. | Light and Darkness,                  | 25    |
| 12. | Our Baby,                            | 28    |
| 13. | Trust,                               | 30    |
| 14. | All for Him,                         | 32    |
| 15. | A Day with Jesus                     | 33    |
| 16. | The Precious Word,                   | 35    |
| 17. | The Answered Prayer                  | 36    |
| 18. | Seeds,                               | 38    |
| 19. | He Calleth for Thee,                 | 40    |
| 20. | Out and Under,                       | 42    |
| 21. | His Jewels,                          | 44    |
| 22. | Only a Step,                         | 47    |

## CONTENTS.

|     |                              | PAGE. |
|-----|------------------------------|-------|
| 23. | CANAAN,                      | 49    |
| 24. | GRAVEN ON HIS HANDS,         | 51    |
| 25. | REFLECTED LIGHTS,            | 53    |
| 26. | FEAR NOT,                    | 55    |
| 27. | PEN PICTURES,                | 57    |
| 28. | THE INDWELLING LORD,         | 63    |
| 29. | THE KING'S JEWEL,            | 65    |
| 30. | HIS WAY IS BEST,             | 67    |
| 31. | CHOOSING,                    | 69    |
| 32. | OUR SUNSET HOUR,             | 70    |
| 33. | THAT PERFECT SONG,           | 72    |
| 34. | EXCEEDING GLAD,              | 75    |
| 35. | POMEGRANATES AND BELLS,      | 76    |
| 36. | FROM SUFFERING TO GLORY,     | 78    |
| 37. | BUSY HERE AND THERE,         | 82    |
| 38. | PRAISE,                      | 84    |
| 39. | TRUSTING; FOR WHAT?          | 87    |
| 40. | CAN NO ONE GO WITH ME?       | 89    |
| 41. | LEAVE IT THERE,              | 91    |
| 42. | SHILOH,                      | 93    |
| 43. | FOLLOW THOU ME,              | 94    |
| 44. | HONORED OF THE LORD,         | 96    |

# THE MASTER'S MESSENGER.

## THE LITTLE MESSENGER.

GO, little messenger, go,
 Quickly and quietly go,
  Like bird on wing.
Tell the sweet story of Love,
Angels first came from above,
 Gladly to sing.

Go now, and gently repeat,
Promises precious and sweet,
 All may believe.
Tell all the weary, oppressed,
Of the blest freedom and rest,
 Jesus will give.

Go to the sorrowing heart,
Tenderest comfort impart
 In Jesus' name;
Tell of bright mansions above,
Tell of His wonderful love,
 Ever the same.

Go, to the careless ones speak,
Urge them the Savior to seek,
    Now, while they may;
Erring ones faithfully warn,
Lest they His message still scorn,
    And farther stray.

Speak, and the wanderer win;
And, to souls burdened with sin,
    Lovingly go.
Tell them Christ's blood can atone,
Wash the dark stains, every one,
    Whiter than snow.

Go to the tempted and tried,
Tell them the Savior once died
    Victory to give;
They who in Jesus believe,
May of His fullness receive,
    And in Him live.

Go, little book, in His name,
Whose promise still is the same,
    His cause to bless;
And if some souls thou shalt win
From the dark pathway of sin,
    Great thy success.

## WALKING IN THE LIGHT.

(TUNE—*Are you coming home to-night?*" Gospel Hymns No. 311.) I John 1-7.

ARE you dwelling in the sunshine?
   Are you walking in the light?
Have you been to Christ for cleansing,
Are your garments "always white?"
Do you live each day rejoicing
In His presence and in His smile?
Does He give you conscious victory?
Is He with you all the while?

### CHORUS.

Are you walking in the light?
Are you walking in the light?
Have you fellowship with Jesus,
Dwelling in His sunshine bright?
Are you doing *all* His will?
Is His service your delight?
Does His Spirit ever guide you?
Are you walking in the light?

Are you dwelling in the sunshine?
Though around the clouds may lower,
Though the tempter ever watching
Even now asserts his power;

You may rise above the shadows
And abide in sunshine bright,
You may conquer Satan *always*,
If you're walking in the light.

Are you fully consecrated,
To His service every day?
Do you follow Him each moment,
In the straight and narrow way?
Are you living for His glory?
Doing all things in His might?
Do your words and actions witness
That you're walking in the light?

## REST:

"*His rest shall be glorious.*"—Isa. 11:10.

(TUNE—"*Come.*"  Gospel Hymns No. 309.)

OH, blessed full assurance;
  Oh, rest that Jesus gives,
To one who comes for cleansing,
  And on His word believes,
Heart-sick and very weary,
  With doubts and fears oppressed,
I claimed his precious promise,
  And He hath given rest.

### CHORUS.

Lord, I came to Thee, gladly came to Thee,
Thou didst save me fully; Thou didst make me free.
Oh, the precious flow! yes, I feel, I know,
Jesus' blood now cleanses and makes me white as snow.

  No evil can befall me,
    Encompassed by His love;
  And in severe temptations,
    His wondrous power I prove.
  And daily I'm rejoicing,
    My heart is free from sin,
  How can I wander from Him?
    My Savior reigns within.

Oh, privilege exalted,
To all believers given,
That while on earth we labor,
We live prepared for heaven.
What more could Jesus offer,
To souls by sin oppressed,
Than what His death has purchased?
A glorious, perfect rest.

## THE THREE GIFTS.

FULL of guilt and sadly burdened,
  Weary, all undone,
Came I to the Father, asking
Pardon through His Son;
Came, a prodigal, repenting,
With my load of sin;
He forgave me, fully, freely,
Took the wanderer in:
Welcomed me with great rejoicing,
He, my Lord and King,
Placed on me most costly raiments,
On my hand, His ring.


Full of vile, inbred corruption,
Lord, I come to Thee,
Asking for that priceless treasure;
Spotless *purity*.
It is given.  O'er me freely
Flows the crimson flood;
I am washed, made pure and holy,
In His precious blood.
On my way I go, rejoicing,
Filled with love and praise,
In His dear, delightful service,
Spending all my days.

Once again a suppliant, coming,
Bowing low this hour,
Feeling all my human weakness,
Asking now for *power*.
Power to keep his whole commandment;
Power to do and dare;
Power to boldly speak for Jesus,
Praise Him anywhere;
And *again* 'tis freely given
Even while I call,
While I claim the precious promise,
Plead His " shall " and " all."

Pardon, purity and power,
Blessed heaven born three,
By the Father, Son and Spirit,
Given unto me.
Was a better, brighter trio,
E'er to mortal given?
On unworthy me, bestowing
Foretaste sweet of heaven.
Then with heart and voice extolling
Through the coming days,
Father, Son and Holy Spirit,
Ever will I praise.

## SON OR SERVANT, WHICH?
### Luke XV, 11 to 24.

OH yes, you have heard the old story,
   And you say that to life it is true,
For long since in the years of your folly,
   *You* once was a prodigal too.
You grew weary of Satan's hard service;
   For death is the wages of sin,
And you longed to return to your Father,
   That eternal life you might win.

You remembered the Father's servants,
   With abundance, enough and to spare,
And you said, "I will go to my Father,
   That I may of their portion share."
But when, on the way, He received you,
   And you saw His forgiving face,
Then, for which did you ask, my brother,
   A *son's* or a *servant's* place?

*You* said, "I have sinned against Him;
   I so long have withstood His grace;
And because I am so *unworthy*
   I will ask for a *servant's* place.
I will serve Him with fear and trembling,
   And will strive to faithful be,
That at last, in His heavenly kingdom,
   He, perhaps, will remember me."

The *Father* said, "Bring the *best* garment,
Bring shoes for the travel worn feet,
And hasten, prepare a great supper,
Of the choicest and richest meat;
And let us rejoice and be merry,
Over this my returning one;
The dead is alive, the lost is found;
Then welcome, my dearly loved *son.*"

You saw all these marks of affection,
You knew 'twas your Father's will
You should share in His love and His riches,
But you chose the *servant's* place still.
And all these long years you have served Him
With trembling, slavish fear,
You have mourned o'er your many failures,
With many a sigh and tear.

Think you not you have *grieved* the Father
In *slighting* His wondrous grace?
Do you think you have *honored* Him greatly,
In choosing a servant's place?
Come now to your rightful possessions,
Accept what He offers to you;
Serve no longer with fetters so binding,
But with *filial* love, strong and true.

The Father so tender and gracious
Still is longing His child to embrace,
He knows though you are serving Him daily,
You are not in your rightful place.
He has blessings, rich, full and abiding,
He will give them to you, every one;
Then count yourself no more a *servant*,
But an honored and dearly loved *son.*

## THE CHILD'S ANSWER.

"DID you get a letter mamma?
And there's black around it too:
Mamma, who did write that letter
And send it here to you?

So I told my little daughter,
Of a friend I loved so dear,
And of all the pain she suffered
Through a long and weary year;

"And now, my little Gracie,"
(And I smoothed the dark brown head)
"This letter comes to tell me
The friend I love is dead."

"No, she is *not* dead, dear mamma,
Why, you *forget*, you know,
Your friend is now with Jesus,
And He makes her white as snow."

Again unto a "little one,"
The Master has revealed,
What from the older, wiser minds,
Has often been concealed.

Oh, darling little three-year-old,
How little do you know,
The wondrous meaning of those words,
" He makes her white as snow."

Yet, precious little comforter,
The simple words you say,
Has led my faith beyond the tomb
To the true and living way.

Oh, when we part with loved ones,
In the valley *we* call death,
Could we look beyond the shadows,
With Childhood's simple faith,

We would hush our vain repinings,
And our tears would cease to flow,
When we know " They are with Jesus
And he makes them white as snow."

## SANCTIFIED AND SATISFIED.

I HAVE been to Christ for cleansing;
   In the fountain deep and wide,
I have plunged; His Spirit whispers,
   Sanctified.
Now my heart with joy is singing,
Dwelling close to Jesus' side,
In His love I'm sweetly resting
   Satisfied.

Consecrated, soul and body,
For His service set aside,
All I have upon the Altar
   Sanctified.
Taking all that Jesus offers,
Every needful want supplied,
All my hopes and earnest longings,
   Satisfied.

Emptied all my sinful nature,
Hatred, unbelief and pride,
Self all conquered, Jesus keeps me
   Sanctified.
Filled with all his glorious fullness,
Wanting nothing else beside,
Loving, trusting; every moment
   Satisfied.

Satan and his hosts assail me,
In my Savior's cross I hide,
Hear again his blest assurance,
 "Sanctified."
Should the storms of life o'ertake me,
Raging sea and angry tide,
Christ is with me, still I'm resting
 Satisfied.

Savior, may I ever linger
Near Thy wounded, bleeding side,
May Thy Holy Spirit keep me
 Sanctified,
Till with Thee and holy angels,
I shall ever more abide;
'Till I wake in Thine own likeness,
 Satisfied.

## THE ANCHOR WITHIN THE VEIL.

Heb. 6, 19. (TUNE: *"Drifting with the Tide."*)

WE are out upon Life's ocean,
  Driven, helpless, towards the shore;
Dark the dreaded storm-cloud lowers,
Loud the angry billows roar.
Hark! the breakers are before us,
As we drift before the tide:
Only one strong Hand can save us,
He, alone, our bark can guide.

> Cast the anchor, sure and steadfast,
> Quickly cast; within the veil,
> Let it touch the Rock of Ages.
> Blessed Rock, that ne'er shall fail.

Just before there lies a harbor,
Wondrous beautiful and fair,
Thither is our Pilot steering,
He would anchor safely there.
Now we mount the foaming billows,
Now the raging waves o'er-whelm;
Think you we'll outride the tempest?
Will the ship obey the helm?

Ah! the fog and mists are rising,
And the harbor fair is seen;

Smiling skies, and rippling waters
Laving shores of varied green.
But the cliffs and hills surround it,
Standing out in bold relief.
And direct across the entrance,
Lies the sand-bar—Unbelief.

Yet there is a narrow channel,
Leading to that haven blest,
Where the weary, storm-tossed mariner,
May in peace and safety rest.
But the *heavy-laden* vessel
Cannot pass that narrow strait;
Cast we *sin* and *self* behind us,
While outside the bar we wait.

Following *Faith's* blessed cable,
Soon the treacherous bar is past:
Now we join the gladsome chorus,
Praise the Lord! in port at last.
Balmy breezes wafts us shoreward,
Bright and clear the sky above,
*This* is perfect rest and safety,
Blessed haven, Perfect love.

Precious Faith, the harbor gaining,
Blessed Hope, within the veil;
Perfect Love, all else excelling,
It shall never, never fail.

## LIGHT AND DARKNESS.

*"And God divided the light from the darkness."* -Gen. 1:4.
*"And there shall be no night there."* —Rev. 22:5.

IN the earliest stage of creation,
  God spake: and behold it was light.
Then, in His omnipotent wisdom,
He divided the day from the night,
And by His own word, strong and mighty,
He completed the glorious plan;
And last in that wondrous creation,
Most wondrous of all, made He man.


Man, fresh from the hand of his Maker,
Pure, holy; Jehovah's delight,
In God's glorious image created
And dwelling in His own light.
This was his estate: but too quickly
Came Sin, with its poisonous breath,
And instead of the sunshine and gladness,
Was sorrow and darkness and death.


Ah! who can describe *all* the anguish,
That came with that darkness of night?
Yet, through the thick gloom and the blackness,
Came a gleam of God's infinite light;

That gleam brought the wonderful promise,
That night should not *always* remain:
Not always the weeping and sighing,
Not always the anguish and pain.

Still the shadows and light intermingle
O'er each page of the sacred word,
Until darkness and death are conquered
At the tomb of a risen Lord.
Yes; our Lord, our Light *has* arisen,
Bringing healing and peace and rest;
But men, in their poor, willful blindness,
*Love* shadows and darkness the best.

Long since had His glorious brightness,
Chased the shadows and darkness away;
Long since had we dwelt in His presence,
And rejoiced in Millennium day,
Would men choose light rather than darkness,
Would they yield to the Father's will;
They *will not*: and so the dark shadows
With the sunshine are mingling still.

There is no path uncrossed by the shadows;
No brow all unclouded by care;
No life, be it ever so joyous,
But *some* sorrow, *some* darkness is there.
Even those who live close to the Master,
Who walk in His own blessed light,
Find weariness, suffering, sighing;
Find the shadows of death and of night.

But again will the edict be sounded,
And night will no longer remain,
Where the King in His wondrous beauty,
In His power and His glory shall reign.
He will gather the mists and the shadows,
And banish them far from His sight;
And naught that offendeth shall enter
That city where cometh no night.

Then where will *you* be, sister, brother?
Redeemed by His blood and made white,
Or banished far, far from his presence,
In the blackness and horror of night.
Would you dwell in His glorious presence?
In His sunshine, resplendent and bright?
Then yield now your heart to your Savior,
And *to-day* turn from darkness to light.

## OUR BABY.

*(Written for parents who have parted with dear little ones.)*

SHE has left us, little darling,
  Gone, with all her baby charms;
Safe and happy, her sweet spirit
Dwelleth in the Saviour's arms.

Laughing bright eyes, closed to earth love,
Smooth and cold the marble brow;
Dimpled, restless little fingers,
Folded, very quiet, now.

Little lips so sweet and rosy,
Moaning through the hours of pain,
Silent now; so white and waxen,
Smile upon us once again.

Darling, precious little baby;
Like a lily-bud so fair,
Plucked before earth's storms could blight it,
Safely sheltered ' over there.'

Ah, our hearts were very selfish,
And we thought her ours alone,
'Till the Master claimed the jewel;
Only took what was his own.

Yes, *our* tender, clinging earth love,
Fain would keep her *always* here,
We would make this world our heaven,
Clasping close our treasures dear.

But the Father draws us heavenward,
With Love's cord of silken strands;
One end, where our faith can grasp it,
The other held by baby hands.

Oh, our Father, draw us gently,
With that golden cord of love;
Lead us on through life's dark changes
To our better home above.

## TRUST.

I AM learning each day a sweet lesson
        Of perfect trust ;
Not blindly obeying the Master
        Because I must,
But, leaning my head on His loving breast
And resting content—for He knoweth best.

If far up the hillside I journey,
        Where all is bright,
Or, in the dark valley I linger
        And see no light,
In sunshine or darkness I trust Him still;
In me He's fulfilling His own perfect will.

He showers such countless blessings
        Along my way,
He shows me so much of His glory,
        While here I stay,
That, trusting in Him I would still abide,
Safe, happy, contented, what e'er betide.

'Tis true that He sometimes sends trials,
        But they are small;
And, Oh, the sweet joy of His presence
        Out weighs them all.
And safe in the arms of His love I rest,
Content that these trials for me are best.

Sometimes the tempter assails me
      With doubts and fears,
And tells of the sorrows and trials
      In coming years,
Of drought and famine, of heat and cold;
Then holds up the world with its glitter and gold.

But what is this world and its glory,
      To Christ, my Lord?
What harm can befall while I'm resting
      On His own Word?
His wonderful comforter dwelling within,
Defies all the powers of darkness and sin.

Dear Lord, I would clasp still closer
      My hand in Thine;
Each day deeper drink of the fountain
      Of love divine.
Then, though earth clouds gather and storms increase,
I am kept in Thine own exceeding peace.

## ALL FOR HIM.

LET your life be *all* for *Jesus*,
Every action, word and thought
For His glory, who your ransom
With such fearful sufferings bought.
*All* for Jesus? Yes, He claims all:
Gladly now your offering bring;
In your inmost heart enthrone him;
Let Him reign, your Lord, your King.

## A DAY WITH JESUS.

BEGINNING the day with Jesus,
　Pausing a while to pray
That with all its unknown duties
　It may be a gladsome day.

Planning the work for the morning;
　Knowing each hour will bring
New tasks, which I take so gladly,
　Direct from the hands of my king.

Giving my Master's message
　To one who has grieved Him long,
Cheering the weary, sad one,
　With a loving word or a song.

Doing *all things* for His glory;
　No matter how great or how small;
Knowing He claims every service,
　Knowing *He cares* for it all.

Bringing my work in the evening,
　Laying it down at His feet,
Praying whatever it lacketh
　*His love* will make it complete.

*Ending* the day with Jesus,
When alone, I my Savior meet,
Like the tired but happy children,
I rest in His love, so sweet.

*This* is a day with Jesus;
Thus doth He lead me along,
Through the beautiful valley of blessing;
The valley of praise and of song.

And I pray that as each day endeth,
As I pause, at the set of sun,
Far down in my heart's deep center,
I may hear His whisper "Well done."

## THE PRECIOUS WORD.

A MOTHER'S gift to her darling girl,
In the Spring-time of her life,
When hopes are bright and her heart is light,
And the future with joy seemed rife.
'Twas a mother's love, chose *this* gift, above
All others, abiding, sure;
When hopes have fled, when joys are dead,
This " Word " shall still endure.
Its pages shine, with light divine,
Leading on to heaven and God;
Its precepts bright, will guide aright,
In the way all saints have trod;
Its promises, too, all proved and true,
Are wonderful, precious sweet.
Then let it guide, and what e'er betide,
We at last in heaven will meet;
'Tis your mother's prayer when we gather there,
You may stand in Christ complete.

## THE ANSWERED PRAYER.

[Two little brothers, Edward and Casler Boardman, aged eight and five years, were burned to death at their home in Nevada City, California, July 24th, 1882. They had been put to bed by their mamma, who, leaving them in charge of a servant, went out for an hour, to return and find her home in flames, and her little ones unrescued.]

"Now I lay me down to sleep,"
 Mother hear your dear ones praying;
"I pray the Lord my soul to take,"
 Infant lips are sweetly saying.
 Oh, how soon the prayer was answered:
 One short hour in dreamland sweet,
 Then, with saints and angels, bowing
 Joyous at their Savior's feet.

"Kiss me just once more, dear mamma,"
 Soft white arms are round her pressed,
"Now, good-by, until the morning;"
 Mamma's darlings sweetly rest.
 Rest in childhood's blissful slumber,
 Never thought of danger near,
 Soon the cruel flames are raging
 Round their precious forms so dear.

 One short step from earth to heaven,
 What a glorious thought is this;

They were wakened in the morning;
By an angel's loving kiss.
Darling, loving little brothers,
You have traveled hand in hand,
From the peaceful dreams of childhood,
To the blessed glory land.

Can we murmur, though our hearts
Are crushed and bleeding, lone and sad,
When we know *their* ransomed spirits
Are so happy, free and glad?
Father, we, thy sorrowing children,
Bow submissive to Thy will;
Knowing 'tis Thy hand that chastens,
"Tho' Thou slay, we trust Thee still."

## SEEDS.

*"In the morning sow thy seed,"* Ecal. 11-6.

SEEDS, seeds, queer little seeds,
   What are they good for? pray tell;
Take just a few, so tiny and round,
Scatter them lightly over the ground,
Now see the magical spell.
Up into sunshine, quickly there springs
A wonderful fairy, with tiny green wings,
Out of each little black shell.
Down in the earth goes a little white root,
Up in the air comes a wee little shoot,
Catching the sunshine and dew.
Stretching so eagerly up to the light,
Nodding and bobbing so pretty and bright,
'Till, between me and you,
'Tis strange, but 'tis true,
Golden grain or else weeds,
Have grown from those little wee seeds.

Words, words, only just words,
Spoken so careless and free;
But children think, count well the cost,
A word once spoken cannot be lost,
Though cross or pleasant it be.
Spoken in anger, brings sorrow and pain;
Spoken in love, Oh, the infinite gain!

With either the harvest you'll see.
Guard then your words; speak them with care;
Of idle, proud, lying, profane words, beware,
*They* bring a sure crop of *weeds*.
Earnest, brave, cheerful words, faithful and true,
Kind, gentle, helping words, loving words, too,
These are bright little seeds,
Which, if followed by deeds,
Like sweet flowers will grow,
Sending gladness where ever they go.

## HE CALLETH FOR THEE.

*"The Master is come, and calleth for thee."*—John xi : 28.

H E calleth for thee.
Yes, Christian, He calls thee, thy vows to renew;
He calls thee to service, whole-hearted and true;
He calls thee all things for *His glory* to do.
   He calleth for thee.

He *calleth* for thee.
He *may* call to pastures where still waters flow,
Where sunbeams are sparkling and sweet flowers grow,
He *may* call, perchance, where the stormclouds bend low.
   Yet he calleth for thee.

He calleth for *thee*.
Wilt thou follow Him fully, thy Lord, crucified,
In His own perfect love to rest and abide,
Ever heeding His voice, pressing close to His side,
   When He calleth for thee?

*He calleth for thee.*
Now hasten, Oh, Christian, thy Master to meet,
Bringing *all* thy possessions to lay at His feet,
And accept His salvation, full, perfect, complete,
   As He calleth for thee.

He *calleth* for thee.
Though now in the desert of sin thou dost roam,
He is waiting to welcome thee now to thy home.
Yes, sinner, to-day the dear Master is come
   And calleth for thee.

*He* calleth for thee.
Many times has he called; in thy childhood bright,
And often, so often in silence of night,
In soft gentle whisper, in power and in might,
    He hath called for thee.

He hath called for thee,
When Death's fingers were laid on one loved the best,
Perhaps 'twas a mother, or the babe at thy breast,
Thou did'st hear a low voice as she passed to her rest,
    "He calleth for thee."

He calleth for *thee*.
Hast thou answered the call? Why longer delay?
Why turn from His love and His mercy away?
Oh, come to Him now, for even *to-day*
    He calleth for *thee*.

*He calleth for thee.*
'Tis the very last summons: though often before
He has called thee in love, He will call thee no more.
The *Master* is gone, 'tis the *Judge* at the door,
    And He calleth for thee.

*He calleth for thee.*
And meet Him thou must, thou can'st not evade;
But, if on thy Savior thy sins are all laid,
Thou can'st meet Him with joy, and go undismayed
    When He calleth for thee.

## OUT AND UNDER.

(TUNE: "*Only an Armor Bearer*." Gospel Hymns, No. 82.)

OUT on the promises, boldly I stand,
Jesus' own promises, Oh, they are grand;
Out on the promises, under the blood,
Cleansed and made pure in that blest crimson flood.
Glorious Salvation, so full and so free!
Glory to Jesus, He sanctifies me.

Out on the promises; wonderful, sure;
His own precious word, it for aye shall endure;
Under the blood, its bright glory I see,
Just now, in its power, it flows over me.
Praise Him, Oh praise Him; the Savior is mine,
Glorious fullness of love all divine.

Out on the promises, faithful and true,
Out where His Spirit my heart can renew.
Under the blood: Oh, the estatic bliss!
Surely a foretaste of heaven is this.
Are *greater* joys known to angels above?
A sinner redeemed by His infinite love.

Out from the world, its allurements and snares,
Out from my doubtings, my fears, and my cares,
Under His shadow securely to rest,
Led by His hand who loves me the best.
Blessings and mercies o'erwhelm as a flood,
While out on the promises, under the blood.

Out on the promises, doing His will,
Looking to Him His own word to fulfill,
Under the blood, where the blest precious flow,
Washes and keeps me, "e'en whiter than snow."
Ever I'll praise Him, all glory to God,
I'm out on the promises, under the blood.

## HIS JEWELS.

*And they shall be mine,— When I make up my jewels.—*
Mal. 3-17.

WE were sitting together at twilight,
'Twas the hour we met to pray,
Just a few young girls who had started,
Together the heavenly way.

But two of our number were absent,
Sweet Ella and Inez fair;
I glanced at their places and wondered,
Why they should fail to be there.

And we sat and talked in the gloaming
Till, down through the quiet skies,
Came a voice of such wonderful sweetness,
It filled us with mute surprise.

We knew 'twas the voice of the Master,
Who once walked by Galilee,
As with accents gentle and tender,
He whispered, "Lovest thou me?"

I listened to hear the quick answer,
"Yea, Lord; thou *knowest* I do;"
Addie, loving, but timid,
Mary, faithful and true,

Lillie, so strong and courageous,
Clara, so quiet and grave,
Each one, in the gathering shadows,
The very same answer gave.

Again came the voice of the Master;
" How long will you faithful be ? "
And again we answered Him gently,
" Until death, I will follow Thee."

Then down through the shadowy stillness,
Like a grand, exulting strain,
So tender, so full of gladness,
Came that wonderful voice again.

" Then you are *mine*, my jewels;
Now and forever more;
And when I come in my glory,
These gems shall my crown adore.

I listened again for His message,
So real did it all seem,
I woke in surprise;—it was morning,
And behold, it was only a dream.

Many years have passed since I dreamed it,
Yet memory brings it again;
It comes, like a low, sweet cadenze,
Like a beautiful, glad refrain.

I think of those young friends, who gathered
Together, at evening to pray;
Do they still follow close by the Master?
Are they now in the narrow way?

Ah, yes, they are still " His jewels,"
They still His commands obey,
The Master, so loving and gentle
They are following, day by day.

Sometimes they follow Him sadly,
With faltering steps and slow;
Sometimes, all filled with His gladness,
On their homeward way they go.

But two of the number beloved
Have crossed o'er the swelling tide;
Dear Ella and Inez so gentle,
In His glorious presence abide.

In different parts of His vineyard,
The others are laboring still;
To win, by their love for Jesus,
Other souls to obey His will.

At last may the band unbroken
Meet around His great white throne,
And hear His glad, glad welcome
To His jewels, His loved, His own.

## ONLY A STEP.

*Behold the Lord thy God hath set the land before thee, go up and possess it.* Deut. 1-21.

IT is 'only a step' into Canaan,
  Then why do you idly stand?
You are waiting just now on its borders,
You are viewing the "promised land."
The land which was long ago given
To Abraham, faithful and true;
The land which by faith *we* inherit,
"Just over the line," waits for you.

You have eaten the "heavenly manna,"
Its taste is both pleasant and sweet,
You have drank of the "Rock" Christ Jesus,
That has followed your wandering feet;
But *this* is a land of plenty,
Abounding in corn and wine;
Say, will you not cross its borders?
"One step" and it *all* shall be thine.

You have wandered long years in the desert,
You have grieved your dear Lord, day by day,
You've murmured, rebelled and forsook Him,
You have tried every way but *His* way.
Are you tired of sin and its sorrow?
Do you earnestly long to be blest?
Then come unto Him who has promised
"I will give to the weary ones rest."

Take Christ as your perfect salvation;
Believe: you shall surely be blest;
Just take *all* that Jesus has promised,
Just *enter* this land of sweet rest.
Then fear not the strong, walled cities,
And fear not the " Anakims " tall,
Our " Joshua " goeth before us,
Our " Jerichos " surely shall fall.

'Tis *faith* that obtains the possession,
By faith we are kept on our way;
Just trusting Him moment by moment,
Brings victory day after day.
Praise God for this beautiful soul rest,
From inward polution set free;
Praise God for this wondrous salvation
Christ has purchased for you and for me.

## CANAAN.

TWO years, two years in Canaan;
　　Such happy, happy years,
So free from sin's defilement,
　　So free from doubts and fears.
Oh! wondrous glories that round me shine!
　　　　The peace and joy,
　　　　Without alloy!
And the perfect rest that is mine, *is mine!*


I see each day new beauties,
　　In this fair, glorious land,
Its peaceful rivers flowing
　　O'er bright and golden sand.
Its lofty mountains; its valleys fair,
　　　　Where flowers sweet,
　　　　Around my feet,
Fling a rich perfume on the balmy air.


The happy birds are singing
　　In ever fruitful trees,
And low, sweet music floating
　　On every passing breeze.
Quiet mountain shadows cross the plains,
　　　　While sunbeams gleam,
　　　　On fount and stream,
And beauteous spring in this land remains.

Its fruits are rare and lucious,
    Abounding everywhere;
And clear, health-giving fountains
    Are springing freely there.
It has treasures whose value has ne'er been told;
      The unfathomed mines
      With rich ore shine,
Exceeding the far-famed Ophir's gold.

Much land is still before me,
    And daily I explore
Its rising hills and mountains
    And scan its beauties o'er.
The King of the land is my chosen friend;
      We often meet
      In communion sweet,
To tell o'er the joys that will never end.

No more is He "Baali,"     (Hos. 2:16.)
    My Master and my Lord,
'Tis "Ishi" now I whisper,
    A more endearing word.
Such wonderful gifts He on me bestows;
      His own sweet voice
      Bids me still rejoice,
While with His pure love my glad heart glows.

Yes, two bright happy years
    In Canaan have I spent,
And still would I continue
    In this blest land content.
Where my dear Redeemer prepares my way,
      Where glory sublime
      O'er all doth shine,
Yes, here, dear Lord, would I ever stay.

## GRAVEN ON HIS HANDS.

*"Behold, I have graven thee upon the palms of my hands.*—Isa 49-16.

SOUNDING from the sacred pages,
    Lo, a promise sweet I hear;
'Tis the Master's gracious accents:
"I am with thee, do not fear.
Thou shalt not forsaken be;
On my hands I've graven thee."

On His hands! Oh, love most wondrous!
Does He show such love to me?
On those hands, once torn and bleeding,
Can *my* name engraven be?
By His holy word He's spoken,
And that word cannot be broken.

Yes, the cruel nails once piercing,
Those dear hands, so blessed, fair,
And the crimson streams, outgushing,
Set the seal forever there:
Now, behold Him, as He stands,
With my name upon His hands.

Loving hands: so sinless, spotless,
Gentle, tender, great in power,
Filled with blessings, rich, abundant,

Freely given every hour:
I may claim their constant care,
For my name is graven there.

Then why should I fear or falter?
He is with me everywhere,
Guides my feet in pleasant pathways,
Guards with more than mother's care;
Always, evermore the same,
On His hands He bears my name.

Through the "valley of the shadow,"
He will lead to mansions bright;
I shall dwell with His redeemed ones,
Clad in garments clean and white;
Faultless in His sight I'll stand,
I am graven on His hand.

## REFLECTED LIGHT.

THE king of day is departing,
  In clouds of crimson and gold,
O'er all the glad earth reflecting
His glory and beauty untold.

I stand by the window, watching
All nature retire to rest;
While over all spreads that banner
Of crimson, unfurled in the west.

The sky flushes bright and brighter
Then fades to a pale rose pink,
As low in the horizon dropping,
The sun into rest doth sink.

And now in the fading splendor
I see a faint light afar,
Then bright on my vision flashes
The beautiful evening star.

Yes, there in the paling crimson,
A beautiful beaming light;
Fair token of day departing,
Bright herald of coming night.

Its beams shine so calm and steady,
Yet still with a radiance bright,
How can a thing of such beauty
Be only reflected light?

## THE MASTER'S MESSENGER.

The glorious sun has departed,
His bright rays no longer I see,
Yet somewhere I know he is shining,
This star shows his beauty to me.

From thee will I learn a lesson
Oh, beauteous evening star;
Bright shining through darkening shadows,
And sending thy beams afar.

My glorious King in His beauty
The world cannot, *will not* see,
'Tis only in His true disciples
His light will reflected be.

Then let me reflect for His glory,
Pure and unsullied rays;
Perchance some one sadly watching,
My Lord will behold and praise.

Though others may shine far above me,
In radiance all their own,
Be it mine to keep close to my Master,
And shine in *His* light alone.

Shine out through mists and shadows,
Shine brightly while yet I may,
'Till, in the fair courts of His glory,
I shine as a sun for aye.

## FEAR NOT.

Fear not little flock,
'Tis your Father's good pleasure
To give you the kingdom.
That wonderful treasure,
Longed for and expected
By prophets and sages;
But from them withheld
Through long, weary ages.
That treasure is yours, God's own Holy Spirit
Enthroned in the heart; this do we inherit.

Fear not little flock,
Though dark the storm lowers,
Though weary the way,
All shorn of bright flowers;
His spirit within you
Shall make all things bright,
Shall comfort and bless you,
And guide you aright.
He lightens the pathway, dispels all the gloom,
Makes long barren deserts with verdure to bloom.

Fear not little flock,
Though tempted and tried,
Though the world may forsake
And friends may deride,

Though taunted and scorned,
Though suffering loss,
He suffered far more,
Who once died on the cross.
The comforter promised shall be with you still;
All things work for good, though it now seemeth ill.

Fear not little flock,
'Tis your Father's good pleasure
To give you all peace,
And joy without measure.
"Ye all shall be mine,"
The Master has spoken,
His immutable word
Can never be broken.
Fear not little flock, to you shall be given
All needful on earth, and the glories of heaven.

## PEN PICTURES.

[*Written for the Nevada County Sunday School Convention,
October 2, 1884.*]

FRIENDS and teachers: To me has been given a task.
  Why so? do you ask?
  To address this intelligent body in rhyme!
  Believe me, I have had such a time,
   To choose a fit subject.
  But to-day if once more
   You will children become,
And with children's interest in any thing new,
Will patiently wait, I will bring to your view,
Some pictures, perhaps seen before.
And if, in my efforts to thus entertain,
I strengthen some half-formed purpose to-day,
Or cheer some soul, weary-grown in the way,
  My endeavor will not be in vain.

### I.

  Crowding to their places,
  On the Sabbath day,
  Happy, boyish faces,
  Eyes, blue, black and gray.
  Listening while the teacher,
  In earnest tones and grave,

Tells again the story,
How Jesus came to save.
Now strangely awed and silent,
Now bubbling over with fun;
Such restless, roguish mortals!
*This* is picture number one.

## II.

Now alone in secret pleading,
With the Father interceding,
For the precious souls entrusted to her care,
That His love would ever guide them,
That no evil should betide them,
This the theme, the burden of the teacher's prayer.
Laboring on, though daily feeling
Pain and langour o'er her stealing,
Knowing well her earthly race will soon be run;
Eyelids closed and hands at rest,
Folded o'er the quiet breast,
And the faithful teacher's work of love is done.

## III.

In a home of wealth and splendor,
See, a little sufferer lies,
While human skill and wisdom,
With each other vainly vies;
And loving, sorrowing parents
Are watching night and day,
Till at last the blue eyes open,

And they hear their darling say:
"No, you cannot help me, mamma,
*You* do not know the way,
I am passing through the valley,
But beyond is endless day;
'Twas my own dear teacher told me,
'Jesus bids the children come,'
Now, *His* arms are round me, mamma,
*He* will carry Willie home."

### IV.

The canvas turns, and before our view,
Is a picture not altogether new:
A place where laughter and curses mingle,
Where lights are flashing and glasses jingle;
I see in the throng a young boy stand,
With a sparkling wine-cup in his hand;
But see, as he raises it to his lip,
Why that start, e'er he takes the fatal sip?
From that glittering glass there seems to rise,
A sweet, pure face, with such earnest eyes,
And he hears again the words she said,
" Look not on the wine when 'tis bright and red:
For, hidden deep in that sparkling thing,
Is the serpent's bite and the adder's sting."
Untasted he dashes the glass away,
And turns from the place without delay,
And broken far aye is the tempter's snare;
This night is answered the teacher's prayer.

## V.

Far away beyond the ocean,
Under burning, torrid skies,
Where graceful palms are growing,
Where sunny streams are flowing,
While around the mountains rise;
Here, in earnest, youthful vigor,
Counting earthly gain but loss,
Now his childhood lessons heeding,
In the Spirit's power pleading,
Stands a herald of the cross.
He has heard the grand commission,
The "Go ye," of his Lord,
And joy his heart is swelling,
While to darkened minds he's telling,
All the wonders of His word.

## VI.

"Take my voice and let me sing,
Always, only for my King."
Soft and slow with a musical flow,
Fall the words on the ears of a listening throng.
Over again, hear the sweet refrain;
Oh, great is the power of sacred song!
In that manly face you can surely trace,
The boy, who once needed a teacher's prayer;
Now his mission bright, his great delight,
To cheer hearts heavy with sorrow and care.

Angels rejoice when that earnest voice
Rings out for God in glad service given;
When, clear and strong, it floats along,
Guiding souls in the way of right and heaven.

### VII.

'Tis a dark and dreary picture,
Where, behind the prison bars,
A gray haired man is sitting
Deeply marked by sin's dark scars;
And dark despair seems written
On that once noble brow,
As memory, backward pointing,
Compares the *then* with *now*.
But amid the gloom and sadness,
Comes a whisper soft and low;
Words he heard in happy childhood;
" Crimson shall be white as snow."
And the Holy Spirit knocking
At that door so long shut fast,
Through the teacher's lifelong influence
Has an entrance gained at last.

### VIII.

There remaineth yet one more picture,
But my pen refuses to trace
The glory, the beauty, the brightness
Of that bless'd heavenly place,
Where that teacher stands, crowned, rejoicing,

While the glad hallelujahs ring,
And presents her class unbroken,
To her glorified Lord and King.

  *  *  *  *

By and by, when we too shall gather,
In those heavenly mansions so fair,
And with the blood-washed, redeemed ones,
We shall in the triumphs share,
Methinks, amid all the rejoicing,
It will most glorious be,
To say, "Here am I, blessed Master,
And the class Thou didst give to me."

## THE INDWELLING LORD.

*"And the Lord whom you seek shall suddenly come to his temple."*
Mal. 3:1.

COME, blessed Lord to Thy temple,
This is my prayer, my plea,
Come to the heart that awaits Thee,
Come, Lord, abide now with me.
Come, in Thy glorious beauty,
Come, every doubt to dispel,
Come and with sweet tender accents
Whisper, " my child, all is well."

Long was Thy temple defiled,
Tarnished and darkened with sin;
Lord, I would have it made holy,
Spotless and glorious within.
Cast out are now all the idols,
Never to enter again;
Cleanse by Thy blood precious Savior,
Enter, and evermore reign.

Lord, Thou art giving Thy spirit
Freely to others around;
Like a strong wind it is coming,
Coming, with strange rushing sound;
Filling them full of Thy glory—
Wonderful glory and grace—
Love, joy, peace, gentleness, goodness,
Shining from each happy face.

Lord, fill *me* now with Thy glory,
Now, as before Thee I bow;
Come as Thou wilt to Thy temple,
Only, dear Master, come *now*.
Quickly the answer was given,
E'en while I pleaded in prayer,
While I awaited His coming,
*Suddenly* Jesus was there.

Not as the strong rushing whirlwind,
Not as the bright, glowing flame,
But, as the dew, soft and silent,
Into His temple He came.
Came, as the hush of the dawning
When night pales into day,
E'er the first notes of the warblers
Welcomes the sun's earliest ray.

And, with that sweet, holy silence,
Glory came down from above;
Cleansed and made pure was the temple
Filled with his own perfect love.
Lord, Thou art reigning triumphant,
Over my heart as I sing;
Oh! the sweet joy of Thy presence,
Jesus, my Savior, my King.

Can I do aught but adore Him?
Can I keep silent? Nay! nay!
Words fail to tell of His goodness,
Yet will I praise Him for aye.
Unto the King in His beauty,
Glad hallelujahs I'll raise;
Worship, and glory, and honor,
Give to the Ancient of days.

## THE KING'S JEWEL.

THERE is told a story olden,
  How the king of all the earth,
Saw a gem of most brilliant beauty,
Of untold, priceless worth:
And He said. "This beautiful jewel,
Is for earth too bright and fair,
I will take it for My own kingdom,
And will keep it safely there.
I will take it now, while 'tis spotless,
Ere its beauty be marred by a stain;
Lest my enemy, ever watchful,
My jewel should strive to gain."

But the servants, to whom had been given
The care of this precious stone,
Were filled with dismay and sorrow,
When the Master claimed his own.
They said, "We would not withhold it;
'Tis Thine by a double right,
But all too soon Thou hast taken,
Our treasure, our jewel so bright.
We had hoped to cut and carve it,
To polish with loving care,
And, in after years, dear Master,
To present Thee a gem more rare.

"Nay," tenderly spake the Master,
" 'Tis a jewel too precious by far,
Your faithful, but unskilled fingers,
Perchance would its lustre mar.
I have purchased it for My glory,
With a price exceeding gold,
And I want it now in My palace,
That all may its beauty behold.
*I* will carefully cut and polish,
Will grave with *My name* the gem,
And with finest gold will set it
In My royal diadem."


Oh, stricken ones, sorrow-laden,
Let the simple tale I tell,
Lead you nearer the blessed Master,
Who still " doeth all things well."
In the dreary hours of anguish,
His presence alone can cheer,
The hand that now holds your treasure,
Can wipe each fast falling tear.
He promises tenderest comfort,
Your sorrowing hearts to sustain;
And beyond, in His palace glorious,
He will give you your jewel again.

## HIS WAY IS BEST.

WE sing, "His way is best,"
  When music fills the air,
Smooth and straight our pathway lies,
Strewn with flowers sweet and fair;
In the bright and sunny days,
We acknowledge all His ways,
And glad the Father praise,
    His way is best.


We say His way is best,
When, with hearts so brave and strong,
We eagerly haste onward,
Nor think the journey long;
When, His service our delight,
Waiting fields for harvest white,
Seem to beckon and invite
    His way is best.


But can His way be best,
When away from this He calls,
And bids us take a narrow path,
Where some dark shadow falls?
Can we leave the brighter way?
Can we praise Him as we pray
And without a murmur say
    "Thy way is best?"

We *say* His way is best,
But we cannot understand,
We cannot in the darkness
 See the guiding of His hand:
We shrink in sudden fear
From the pathway lone and drear,
And His voice we fail to hear:
　　" My child, 'tis best."

We whisper, " Is it best,
That we should turn aside
And walk where hidden dangers wait
In a darkened way, untried ?"
Oh, feeble faith and small!
Shall not the Lord of all,
Who heeds the sparrow's fall,
　　Know what is best.

We say His way is best,
But we idle must remain,
While others gladly labor
And gather golden grain;
Nay: We need not idly stand,
For e'en a trembling hand
Seeds may scatter or the land:
　　He knoweth best?

Thy way Oh, Lord is best.
Oh, forgive our needless fears,
We know Thy love will lead us
Through all the coming years.
Lord, we clasp our hands in Thine,
And the darkened way shall shine
With a radiance all divine,
　　Thy way is best.

## CHOOSING.

CHILDREN have you chosen Jesus?
    Do you love Him *first* and *best*?
More than father, more than mother,
Love Him more than all the rest?

Do you always try to please Him,
In your work and in your play?
Are your hearts so glad and happy,
In His service every day?

When you hear His name derided,
Do you that dear name defend?
Do you tell them gently, kindly,
That the Savior is *your friend*?

Choose Him, children, choose Him gladly,
Let each heart-door open wide,
And the gentle, loving Savior,
*Now* will enter and abide.

## OUR SUNSET HOUR.

(*Pacific Coast Holiness Association.*)

IT is evening now; over hill and vale
  The cool, quiet shadows of twilight fall,
And the setting sun with its golden ray,
Sheds a halo of glory over all.
'Tis the sunset hour; on the silent air
Voices of prayer and praise arise,
For God's chosen ones, from far and near,
Have come to the evening sacrifice.

From the lofty Sierra's snow-capped hills,
From where orange groves perfume the air,
From the fertile plain with its streams and rills,
From God's first temples so wondrous fair,
From North to South, from East to West,
From crowded city and hamlet small,
To our loving Father's throne on high,
The incense of prayer ascends from all.

Ah! many, to-night, all over the land
Are 'besieging the throne' this quiet hour;
Some, strong in the midst of battle stand,
Some, sorely tried by the tempter's power.
But our loving Father, who knows us all,
And what will be best for every one,
Sends his richest blessings freely down
While yet our petitions are scarce begun.

Oh, blessed hour of communion sweet!
With what holy joy do we gather there,
Our faith united, our hopes are one,
In this beautiful, twilight hour of prayer.
"God bless our cause," and unwavering faith
Claims the blessing we ask in Jesus' name;
"God hasten the day when through all the land
Salvation shall spread as a glowing flame.

"Lord fill our hearts with power divine
To do thy will as angels do;
And grant that thy children every one
May be valiant, faithful, loyal and true.
God bless our leaders; may faith be strong,
As they wage the fight 'gainst the hosts of sin,
And, Oh, from the throngs on the downward road,
May it be their work many souls to win.

"And may thy chosen, thy faithful ones,
In the beauty of holiness praise Thee still;
Serving Thee gladly, day by day,
With perfect heart and upright will.
'Till, grand as the ocean's mighty roll,
The saints below with the saints above,
Shall join in a long triumphant song,
And the theme shall be, 'Redeeming love.'"

## THAT PERFECT SONG.

I HEARD one tell in language grand,
  Of a wonderful scene in a distant land;
A palace of crystal most grand and fair,
And many thousands were gathered there.
For the children had come from far and near,
And wondering throngs were there, to hear
Those bird-like voices   Five thousand strong
Were the children.  And in all that throng,
Not one before had ever heard
Of the song they sang either note or word.
The signal is given: on the listening throng
Bursts the wonderful, grand, triumphant song.
Now rising loud with a pleasing swell,
Now faint and low as a distant bell.
Enraptured they listen; yet not a sound
Of approval disturbs the quiet profound.
Again the song; with strained, eager ear,
They breathless wait, but they fail to hear
One note of discord, one strain too long.
'Tis a grand success !   'Tis a *perfect* song !
In wondering silence they wait again
Till the children finish the thrilling strain,
Then, with one accord to their feet they spring
And with shout and cheer make the arches ring.

  \*    \*    \*    \*    \*    \*

I thought of *another* palace so fair,
And of countless millions who gather there;

## THE MASTER'S MESSENGER.

From far and near they too have come,
From every land they are gathering home.
In the midst of the palace the 'great white throne,'
And on it the High and Holy One;
Around it, all radiant, in spotless white,
Redeemed ones so precious in Jesus' sight.
All nations and ages are gathered there,
But nearest the throne are the children dear;
A song they sing, so sweet and clear,
That angels amazed pause to hear
That melody new, that theme so grand,
As it bursts from the lips of the white-robed band.
" Unto Him who has loved us all praise be given,
From lowest of earth to highest of heaven."
Through the arches of heaven it rolls along,
That beautiful, glorious, *perfect* song.
And down through the sin-polluted air,
Comes an echo faint of that music rare;
We catch a glimpse of that wondrous love
Which brought our Lord from the courts above,
To suffer and die on the cruel tree
To purchase salvation so full and free.
With joy we join the rapturous strain,
And echo it back to heaven again:
" Unto him, our Redeemer from sin's dark plight,
Who has washed us and made us clean and white,
*All* glory, honor and praise be given,
By the saved on earth and the saved in heaven."
And the two songs blending, swell again,
More loud and clear than on Bethlehem's plain,
The angels' song made the heavens ring,

Proclaiming the birth of the infant King.
And onward still shall the chorus roll,
Till His glory shines from pole to pole;
Till every isle of the boundless sea
Shall be filled with His wondrous majesty;
Then, as countless ages roll along,
All men shall join in that perfect song.

## EXCEEDING GLAD.

Matt. 5: 11-12. (Tune: *"Beulah Songs,"* Page 35.)

OH, ye who labor earnestly,
Precious souls for God to win,
Who tell the tidings glorious,
Of salvation from all sin.

CHORUS.

"Blessed are ye when men revile,"
Is the message of your Lord,
"Rejoice and be exceeding glad,
For great is your reward."

What though the world in scorn deride,
And evil speak of you;
Though all men persecute, forsake,
They hated Jesus, too.

"Exceeding glad" well may you be,
Since He your hearts doth fill
With peace and comfort, life and love,
And joy unspeakable.

You know not yet His "great reward,"
Enough it is to be,
Cleansed daily by His precious blood,
Rejoicing, glad and free.

And when, in heavenly mansions fair,
You meet your blessed Lord,
Then from His hand shall you receive
Exceeding great reward.

## POMEGRANATES AND BELLS.

### (Ex. 28, 33-35.)

WHEN within the veil—the holiest,
  Jewish high priest yearly went,
Clad in spotless garments; bearing
  Sin's atonement,—bullock's blood;
Holy mitre, ephod, breastplate,
  Each symbolic meaning told,
Holy robe; and neath its border,
  Pomegranates and bells of gold.

And without, the people, listening,
  Heard the sweet-toned golden bell,
Knew their priest was interceding,
  Knew he lived and all was well.
Then before the congregation
  He appeared; and they behold,
Pomegranates; blue, purple, scarlet,
  Alternate with bells of gold.

We, a royal priesthood, holy,
  Entered now within the veil,
Through the sacrifice once offered,
  Jesus' blood;—it ne'er shall fail;
Are our lips and lives confessing
  *All* the Lord would have us tell?
Double witness—sound and service,
  Pomegranate and golden bell.

Those without are listening, listening,
For our clear-toned bells of gold,
Telling of the blood that cleanseth,
Sweetest story ever told.
Day by day they're waiting, watching,
If in us they may behold
Holy fruits:—love, joy, peace, meekness;
Pomegranates with bells of gold.

Let the bells ring; clearly, sweetly,
Telling of the blood applied,
Of the fount of perfect cleansing,
Opened when the Savior died.
And in joyous, willing service,
Let our lives the story tell,
That the world in us may witness,
Pomegranate and golden bell.

## FROM SUFFERING TO GLORY.

[In memory of Polly Keer Morris; an earnest devoted Christian, who, after months of intense suffering, borne without a murmur, passed peacefully away, to be with Jesus, at her home in Chicago, January 13, 1884. Of her it may truly be said; " None knew her but to love, none named her but to praise."]

SEE the angel-watchers bending o'er the patient sufferer's bed,
Where the grief-bowed loved ones linger till the last faint word is said;
O'er the weary, wasted features spreads a halo all divine,
As the glories of eternity upon her vision shine.
The breath comes faint and fainter; the heart throbs gently cease;
And o'er the pallid features rests His own exceeding peace.
The angel-watchers, who, with joy, at His own will have come,
The liberated spirit take to bear it safely home.

Down through the deep blue ether, hear the gladsome music swell,
The blessed, heavenly music her spirit loved so well:
Listen to the angel chorus, the glorious, thrilling strain,
We only catch an echo of that wondrous sweet refrain.
Now it louder swells and clearer as they mount the vaulted sky

And wing their way with gladness to the Father's home
    on high.
Now the strains come slower, sweeter; they are nearing
    heaven's gate,
Where many, many loved ones in glad expectance
    wait.


Open, open gates of glory, throw your pearly portals
    wide,
That the patient, much-loved sufferer now may enter
    and abide;
Pure and white her once soiled garments, plunged be-
    neath the crimson flood,
Naught of her own merit pleading, this her passport
    "Jesus' blood."
Open, then, the gates of glory, let the ransomed spirit in,
To that bright and glorious city, where, forever free
    from sin,
Free from pain and care and sorrow, with angelic be-
    ings bright,
She shall spend a long eternity of infinite delight.


See her now as she approaches the beauteous "great
    white throne;"
See the Savior as he greets her, His well-beloved, His
    own;
See Him place the jeweled diadem upon her low-bowed
    head,
And with sweet and tender accents hear the words of
    welcome said.

Now the host of loved ones throng around, each waiting her embrace,
But *first* in all that heavenly band she sees her father's
 face.
Oh! the joy, the joy of meeting in that land where fall
 no tears,
The father she has longed to see through many weary
 years.

And others press around her with eager, out-stretched
 hand,
Some very, very dear ones she had known in distant
 land;
Tho' on earth by ocean severed, they have walked the
 same blest way,
And now they meet in heaven, in the realms of endless
 day.
And the little ones are gathering, those faces bright and
 sweet,
All beam with joy ecstatic as their "teacher" now they
 greet.
Though here no children called her by that dearest,
 sweetest name,
There many precious little ones a mother's love will
 claim.

Ah, truly wrote a sainted one\* in pleasing, rhyming
 spell,
That the beauties of our heaven no mortal tongue can
 tell.

---

\* F. R. Havergal.

We cannot view its glories, there is a veil between,
And the pen but faintly traces what the eye has never seen.
Blessed gleams of glory reach us as we journey on our way,
And soon we too will reach the gates that lead to endless day.
Then, when our earth-born sorrows are forever safely passed,
We shall see, not dimly, darkly, but "face to face at last.

## BUSY HERE AND THERE.

### I. Kings 20:40.

HAVE you not heard the story of old,
  The son of the prophet, to King Ahab told?
Of the Syrian captive left to his care,
And while he was busy here and there,
The captive was gone, he knew not where.
And King Ahab answered when he heard it all,
"As thou hast spoken, so stand or fall."

May not the parable old but true,
Suggest a lesson to me and to you?
Chances for service, so grand and so rare,
Like the Syrian captive, are left to *our* care,
But we are *so busy*, just here and there;
Absorbed in earth's trifles we're hurrying on,
And when we have *leisure*, the captive is gone.

Oh, soldiers of Jesus! shall we idly stand,
While sin and its allies are still in the land?
Have we no captive for Jesus to-day
When Satan is leading so many away?
Shall we not win *just one* while we may?
Souls all around us immortal and fair,
May be lost while we're busy just here and there.

## THE MASTER'S MESSENGER.

Oh, time is too precious to fritter away:
Life is so short, it may *end* with to-day.
Christ calls for volunteers faithful and true,
To do with their might whatsoever they do;
To rescue the lost, be they many or few.
In His presence, Christians, think you we'll dare
To say "Lord I was busy just here and there."

Seek first *His* kingdom; may this be our care,
To be busy for Jesus, just here and there;
Send His glad message to every land;
Scatter the seed with a bold fearless hand;
Sow by all waters; ne'er idly stand:
Then at his appearing a crown we shall wear,
If for him we're busy, just here and there.

## PRAISE.

All the works of God sing praises
    To His holy name;
Shall not we, His chosen people
    Gladly do the same?
Praise Him ever, ceasing never
All His wonders to proclaim.

Listen to the feathered warblers,
    Loud their anthems raise,
Making hill and wood and valley
    Echo with His praise;
Ever singing, glad notes ringing,
Through the happy summer days.

Tiny flowers lift their petals
    Upwards to the light;
O'er them butterflies, all radiant,
    Hover with delight.
Brooklets dancing, sunbeams glancing,
All around is gay and bright.

Grateful kine at noon reclining
    'Neath the shady trees,
And the hum of busy insects
    Borne on every breeze;
God attending, condescending,
Praise accepts from all of these.

Mighty oceans sound His praises
    As they roll and swell,
Snow-crowned mountains, pointing heavenward,
    Of His goodness tell.
Lightnings flashing, torrents dashing,
Speak His mighty power to quell.


Rain and hail and snow and vapor,
    *All*, His wonders show.
Sun, moon, stars, each in its orbit
    At His bidding go.
All creation, in adoration,
To their Lord and Maker bow.


Angels in the courts of glory,
    Glad their homage bring,
Heaven's arches loud resounding,
    With Hosanna's ring:
  Bow before Him and adore Him,
Worshipping their Lord and King.


And shall we most blest and favored,
    Even silent be?
Shall we raise no note of gladness,
    Father, unto Thee?
While abounding, us surrounding,
All Thy love and care we see.

Let us praise Him while we linger
    From the world apart;
Chide not though some glad one praise Him
    In the busy mart:
Joyous singing, to Him bringing
Homage of a grateful heart.


Ever praise Him, speak His glory,
    Tell it round about;
Loud proclaim His great salvation
    E'en with song and shout.
Through the highways, and the byways,
Let the gladsome sound ring out.


Yes, with loyal heart and loving,
    Praise Him everywhere;
Till, beyond life's lights and shadows,
    In those mansions fair,
Gladsome praise, through endless days,
We with angel hosts shall share.

## TRUSTING FOR WHAT?

YOU say you are *trusting in Jesus*,
    Trusting for what?
For pardon and peace you're believing;
    Praise God for that.
His forgiveness and love are so precious,
    All this is true;
But He who can *pardon* so freely,
    Can *sanctify* too.

You're trusting at last to reach heaven;
    And so you may,
If you follow His Spirit's guidance
    Day after day.
But may not the Christian's heaven
    On earth begin?
May we not walk with Jesus
    All free from sin?    (I John 1:7.)

Will you not trust Christ for cleansing
    This very hour?
Think of His wonderful promise, (Ezek. 36:25.)
    Doubt not His power.
He is so gracious and loving,
    He will fulfill,
In you *all* his good pleasure
    For 'tis his will.    (II. Thess. 1:11.)

Jesus requires your whole service (Mat. 22:37.)
    Faithful and true;
He wants a complete consecration (Rom. 12:1.)
    Naught else will do.
Just bring *all* your treasure and lay it (Matt. 19:21)
    Down at His feet,
Then trusting will be *so* easy
    And rest *so* sweet.

## "CAN NO ONE GO WITH ME."

[The last words of a young girl, a Sabbath School scholar, who died suddenly, without having made any preparation for eternity.]

"CAN no one go with me?" the way is *so* dark,
 No "light in the valley;" no comfort; and hark!
I am nearing the river; I hear the deep roll
Of its dark, swelling current; God pity my soul.
Oh! life is so charming; this world is so fair;
Must I leave it forever? Oh! *must* I go, where
That cold water waits me, those cruel waves toss?
Can no one go with me to help me across?

"Ah, yes, I had heard of this terrible day,
But I was so young, death seemed far away
And life all before me. Light-hearted and free
I lived on; nor heeded Death's warnings to me.
In the midst of my pleasure he hurls his dread dart;
I can feel his cold fingers close, close to my heart;
I am dying, yes, *dying*, I know it is true;
Can no one go with me? can none help me through?

"Go, warn my companions; Oh, let them not come
To where I now stand, on the verge of the tomb,
Looking out in despair on the darkness and night,
With the world and its joys fading fast from my sight.
Oh, tell them of my sad mistake to beware;
*They* still have the time for this hour to prepare;
While I into darkness must go *all alone*;
There's none to go with me, no, not even one.

"They tell me of Christ; that salvation is nigh;
That Jesus has pardoned worse sinners than I:
Not *worse*, I have willfully *slighted* His love,
Have lived *only* for *self*, not for heaven above.
Perhaps He *will* hear my last cry of despair,
Perhaps I may *enter* those mansions so fair,
But now, as I go through Death's valley so drear,
He does not go with me the pathway to cheer."

Oh, why will the young be so thoughtless and gay,
When death comes so soon! seek Christ while you may.
Just now He is calling, just now hear His voice
So tender and loving. Oh, make Him your choice.
Then, early or late should that last summons come,
There'll be light in the darkness, and joy in the gloom,
You will not go *alone* through the deep surging tide,
For Christ will be with you to comfort and guide.

## LEAVE IT THERE.

BURDENED soul, weary
    With thy care,
Take it all to Jesus;
    Leave it there.

Not alone *great* burdens,
    Will He bear,
E'en thy *smallest* trials
    He will share.

Though a tiny burden
    It may be,
Yet it is too heavy
    Far for thee.

Though 'tis small, yet larger
    It will grow,
And its weight increasing
    Bow thee low.

Thou can'st never bear it
    All alone,
Take it to the Strong
    And Mighty One.

He will gladly carry
    *All* thy care,
Only *take* it to Him,
    Leave it there.

To this *willing* Saviour
    Often go.
Tell Him all thy sorrow
    And thy woe.

What would grieve thee sorely
    To reveal
To the hearts around thee,
    *He* can feel.

He thy human weakness
    Knoweth best;
He would give thee, tired one,
    *Perfect* rest.

Take then, *all* thy trials
    Great and small,
At the feet of Jesus
    Leave them all.

Take thy cares but bring them
    Not away,
Leave them with the Master,
    Day by day.

Each day brings new trials
    Of its own:
Take them all to Jesus
    *Every one.*

For the many earth cares
    That annoy,
He gives rest and quietness,
    Peace and joy.

## SHILOH.

*"Until Shiloh come."*—Gen. 49:10.
*"Come unto Me—I will give you rest."*—Mat. 11:28.

WITH prophetic vision seeing,
   Life just ending, almost home,
Hear the aged patriarch saying,
   "Till the promised Shiloh come."

Thou art come, Oh, blessed Shiloh,
   Bringing perfect peace and rest;
Gathering Thy wandering children,
   From the north, the east, the west.

From Judea's hills and valleys,
   Echoing o'er Gennesaret's sea,
We have heard His loving summons,
   "Come poor, weary ones to Me."

We are coming, precious Savior,
   Weary now, by sin oppressed,
Coming to the Fount for cleansing,
   Coming to Thy perfect rest;

Thou wilt cleanse us, Thou hast promised;
   Thou will make our hearts Thy throne,
Rule us with Thy righteous scepter,
   Keep us always, Thine alone.

Thou *art* cleansing, Thou art blessing,
   As we lean upon Thy breast,
Thou art filling us with gladness,
   Thou, *our Shiloh*, Thou, *our rest.*

## FOLLOW THOU ME.

*"What is that to thee? Follow thou Me."*—John 21:22.

YOU who are at ease in Zion,
  Living on in careless pleasure,
Seeking of each other honor,
Grasping only *earthly* treasure,
Great mistakes you now are making,
Fearful risks your soul is taking,
What are all *these* things to thee?
Jesus says, "Follow thou *Me*."

You are making vain excuses
Of what *others* do and say,
Of the throngs who follow Mammon,
Of the few who walk *His* way,
Of the hypocrites, deceivers,
Of the halting, weak believers;
What, Oh soul, is that to thee?
Jesus says, "Follow *thou* Me,"

*Follow* Him, yes, fully, wholly,
Not with faltering steps and slow,
But with loving, loyal purpose,
With your Master gladly go.
Follow Him in joy or sorrow,
Follow Him to-day, to-morrow,
This, Oh soul, He claims of thee,
When He calls, "*Follow* thou Me."

*Choose* to follow Christ your Master,
Your discipleship to prove,
In your life of self-denial,
In your meekness, patience, love.
Follow through Gethsemane's gloom,
To His cross, His death, His tomb;
This he will require of thee,
When he bids thee "Follow Me."

Follow on, still closer pressing
To thy risen Savior's side,
Listening to His faintest accents,
In His presence still abide.
Follow Him while life is given,
Follow Him for *aye* in heaven.
This the *glory* offered thee,
In the summons "Follow Me."

## HONORED OF THE LORD.

"*Them that honor me, I will honor.*"—1 Sam. 2:30.

WHEN to the Lord I humbly came,
  Claiming, through faith in Jesus' name,
A *perfect* cleansing from all sin
And power to *keep* me pure within,
While yielding all unto His will,
And clinging to His promise still,
His Spirit gently whispered then,
"And will you consecrate your pen?"

Yes, gladly; 'tis no longer mine,
My life, time, talents, all are Thine;
Then take my pen and let it prove
To others all Thy wondrous love.
Oh, grant that it may ever trace
The glorious fulness of Thy grace,
And ' full salvation ' still proclaim,
To those who feebly own Thy name.

Then the dear Lord on me bestowed
A gift. In rhyming measures flowed
My thoughts; and this the pleasing theme,
"Christ's power so *fully* to redeem."
And so I wrote the thoughts *He* sent,
And quickly through the land they went.
I now begin, though with surprise,
My childhood dreams to realize.

## THE MASTER'S MESSENGER.

Yes, I had wished an Author's fame,
But, seeking for *myself* a name,
I found it not.   But when alone
I sought *His* glory, not my own,
Oh, then He *greatly honored* me.
And so I write, and hope to be,
A messenger for my dear Lord,
To tell in rhyme His precious word.

And now the closing page is filled;
And gladly to my Lord I yield
This, my first book.   Oh, may each page
Speak for *His glory*.   Encourage
*Some* soul to seek the King's highway,
Which brighter grows to perfect day.
This my exceeding great reward,
To lead souls *nearer* to the Lord.

www.ingramcontent.com/pod-product-compliance
Lightning Source LLC
Chambersburg PA
CBHW031121160426
43192CB00008B/1074